Little RIDDLERS

Middlesex Poets

Edited By Machaela Gavaghan

First published in Great Britain in 2018 by:

Young Writers
Remus House
Coltsfoot Drive
Peterborough
PE2 9BF
Telephone: 01733 890066
Website: www.youngwriters.co.uk

All Rights Reserved
Book Design by Ashley Janson
© Copyright Contributors 2018
SB ISBN 978-1-78896-766-2
Printed and bound in the UK by BookPrintingUK
Website: www.bookprintinguk.com
YB0372K

FOREWORD

Dear Reader,

Are you ready to get your thinking caps on to puzzle your way through this wonderful collection?

Young Writers' Little Riddlers competition set out to encourage young writers to create their own riddles. Their answers could be whatever or whoever their imaginations desired; from people to places, animals to objects, food to seasons. Riddles are a great way to further the children's use of poetic expression, including onomatopoeia and similes, as well as encourage them to 'think outside the box' by providing clues without giving the answer away immediately.

All of us here at Young Writers believe in the importance of inspiring young children to produce creative writing, including poetry, and we feel that seeing their own riddles in print will keep that creative spirit burning brightly and proudly.

We hope you enjoy riddling your way through this book as much as we enjoyed reading all the entries.

CONTENTS

Ark John Keats Academy, Enfield

Ayush Purbhoosing (6)	1
Darcie Willcox (6)	2
Toba Joel Okundalaiye (5)	3
Christian Corrales Sweeney (6)	4
Emily Jolley (6)	5
Helin Soylemez (6)	6
David Toby Okorogu (6)	7
Emmanuel Somto Okorogu (6)	8
Nazli Kendir (5)	9
Levi Benjamin (6)	10
Elad Danquah (6)	11
Adam El-Haimer (6)	12
Aleyna Boran (6)	13
Kaiden Campbell (6)	14
May Aaliyah Nguyen (6)	15
Elif Agday (6)	16
Maysa Testore (6)	17
Erblin Temaj (5)	18
David Oluwasemilore Elegbede (6)	19
Clayton Zefi (5)	20

Buckingham Preparatory School, Pinner

Aaran Amey (6)	21
Hassan Faisal (7)	22
Hayder Al Mushcab (7)	23
Jerome Oberoi (7)	24
Anish Kuchangi (6)	25
Neel Sinha (7)	26
Rishabh Ray (6)	27
Shrey M Vadera (7)	28
Maks Pociask (7)	29
Mohsin Faisal (7)	30
Shivesh Joshi (7)	31
Ram Tyagi (7)	32

Guru Nanak Sikh Academy, Hayes

Sneha Khurana (7)	33
Divjot Singh (7)	34
Anaikam Sethi (6)	35
Mehtaab Malhi (7)	36
Saihaj Singh Malhotra (6)	37
Ayush Kumar (6)	38
Yafi Muhammad Ajeebkhan (7)	39
Anshneev Kaur Arora (6)	40
Divleen Kaur Dang (5)	41
Avleen Kaur Virdee (6)	42
Reet Kaur Chawla (6)	43
Bhagat Singh Vig (6)	44
Eknoor Gill (6)	45
Prabveer Singh Sachdeva (5)	46
Pinak Mistry (7)	47
Divjot Singh Khurana (7)	48
Rajdeep Kaur Jheeta (6)	49
Nanta Singh Matharu (7)	50
Gurleen Dhaliwal (6)	51

Harefield Infant School, Harefield

Summer Byatt (5)	52
Harry John Smith (6)	53
Emilia Peliova (6)	54
Lily May Kane (6)	55
Molly Moles (6)	56
Zayn Kashif-Munir (6)	57
Maisie Hayward (5)	58

Ruby Jockel (5)	59
Lilly-Rayne Nuth (6)	60
Gustas Bartkevicius (5)	61
Katie Charlotte Harris (6)	62
Molly Redfern (5)	63
Amelia Carey (6)	64
Jake Phillips (6)	65
Betty Ann Shine (6)	66
Olly Hughes (6)	67
Francesca Sofflet (6)	68
Ronny Ford (6)	69
Isabella Gardner (6)	70
Tyler Josh Sim (6)	71
Christianna Barnes (6)	72
Hany Abusaid (6)	73
Harry Seymour (6)	74
Evie Walford (5)	75
Dawsyn Pheney (6)	76
Leo Clements (6)	77
Mia Castro-Hendley (6)	78
Riley Huntington (6)	79
Lily King (6)	80
Scarlett Brimble (6)	81
Ethan Kerry-Wallington (6)	82
Ben Edwards (6)	83
Harley Stokes (6)	84
Esra Abusaid (6)	85

Hermitage Primary School, Uxbridge

Emilia Autumn Elizabeth Dennis (6)	86
Zain Rahman (6)	87
Maryam Zelamal (6)	88
Thomas Santiago Valera (6)	89

Newton Farm Nursery, Infant & Junior School, South Harrow

Ayushka Shetty (6)	90
Sunny Dhanji Khetani (5)	91
Brajesh Pradhan (6)	92
Amaal Mamdani (6)	93

Sagana Satkunarajah (6)	94
Jasmin Patel (6)	95
Samir Yaqubi (6)	96
Vianna Rabadia-Coll (5)	97
Zara Patel (6)	98
Aryan Chaudhary (6)	99
Simran Kalra (5)	100
Jeeya Prasai (6)	101
Sahasra Myneni (6)	102
Maryam Shifan (6)	103
Sivika Arulkumaran (5)	104
Sophia Iqbal (6)	105
Jasmin Aarushi Patel (6)	106
Dhanvi (6)	107
Akanksha Vydyam (6)	108

Oakington Manor Primary School, Wembley

Dalia Al-Jubouri (7)	109
Diyani Vekeria (6)	110
Aksheran Ananthaseran (7)	111
Cianna Howe-Young (7)	112
Ihsaan Agyeman-Owens (6)	113
Maximilian Paulo Lule (7)	114
Farhan Ahmad Saiady (6)	115
Kitty Lauter (6)	116
Aysia Demetrio Patel (6)	117
Romario Jozef Scoon (7)	118
Amelia Sarban (7)	119
Elijah Vernalls (6)	120
Sarah Dumitriu (7)	121
Mohemed Ahmad (7)	122
Dev Shaju Nair (6)	123
Asma Hassan (7)	124
Raine Denae Robinson (7)	125
Samira Said (5)	126
Abdullahi Ahmad (6)	127

St James' CE Primary School, Enfield

Samaiah Marlene Bent (6)	128
Rhema Zoe Banful (6)	129

Emily Tuffour (6)	130
Isabel Ibrahim (6)	131
Malakai Amali Rowland (6)	132
Chigozie Jessy Anyanwu (6)	133
Evangelina Duzgun (6)	134
Naomi Oprer (6)	135
Ocean-Maxime Asiamah (6)	136
Ayla-Rae (6)	137
Arav Guddah (6)	138
Audrey Tawiah (5)	139
Ademidola Akarakiri (5)	140
Taylan Kiani (6)	141
Vasianna Dussard (6)	142
Joel Jojo (5)	143

St Mary's CE School, Norwood Green

Millan Babrah (7)	144
Abigail Roman (7)	145
Parisa Rizvi (7)	146
Ilaria Bhatti (7)	147
Giovanna Armond (7)	148
Arran Singh Reehal	149
Summer Zahra Rizvi (7)	150
Harry Alan Burns	151
Daniel Joshua Wilson-Paz Sotomayor (7)	152
Jessica Toms (7)	153
Niam Bangar (7)	154
Alisha Patel	155
Mya Belle Spencer	156
Renu Kaur Virdee (7)	157
Jarvis Isaac Sylvester Dennis (7)	158
Dhruv Jahnaid Vansanten (7)	159
Anika Jagota (7)	160
Richard Clarke (7)	161
Eleanor Hamlyn (6)	162
Jeevan Singh Sanghera (6)	163

THE POEMS

Blue Vroom

Blue vroom, blue vroom,
I have wheels big and round.
Blue vroom, blue vroom,
I have lots of windows.
Blue vroom, blue vroom,
I have four doors.
Blue vroom, blue vroom,
I make the sound *beep, beep!*
Blue vroom, blue vroom,
I take people to places.
Blue vroom, blue vroom,
What am I?

Answer: A car.

Ayush Purbhoosing (6)
Ark John Keats Academy, Enfield

What Am I?

I like to eat the leaves from the top of the highest trees.
I have long, wobbly legs and knobbly knees.
I have the longest, tallest, bendiest neck in all of the jungle.
I have a thin tail that swishes.
I am covered in yellow and brown spots from head to toe.
What am I?

Answer: A giraffe.

Darcie Willcox (6)
Ark John Keats Academy, Enfield

Flash

I am fast.
Watch me go fast around the corner.
I come in different colours and sizes.
My sound is *vroom, vroom!*
Kids like to play with me and adults like to drive me.
I am bright and shiny.
I am so flash.
What am I?

Answer: A car.

Toba Joel Okundalaiye (5)
Ark John Keats Academy, Enfield

What Are We?

We can be big or we can be small.
We can go fast, slow or not move at all.
We have many different colours and shapes.
We can be found all around the world.
Vroom, vroom, let's go!
What are we?

Answer: Cars.

Christian Corrales Sweeney (6)
Ark John Keats Academy, Enfield

Gentle Giant

I like to flap my very large ears.
I am the largest animal on land.
I never, ever forget.
My body is ginormous.
I am very grey and wrinkly.
I have an exceedingly long trunk.
What am I?

Answer: An elephant.

Emily Jolley (6)
Ark John Keats Academy, Enfield

Play, Play

I am friendly.
I love children.
I am cuddly.
Everyone likes to teach me.
I love to play.
I love to eat bones.
I love to bark at thieves.
I love to protect my family.
What am I?

Answer: A dog.

Helin Soylemez (6)
Ark John Keats Academy, Enfield

What Am I?

I bring warmth and brightness.
I come out in the morning.
I go down in the evening.
I am natural.
I can't be covered.
I stay longer in the summer.
I am up there.
What am I?

Answer: *The sun.*

David Toby Okorogu (6)
Ark John Keats Academy, Enfield

I Have A Lot Of Fans

I can make my fans cry.
I can make my fans laugh.
I am known in the whole world.
Sometimes you lose, sometimes you win.
There are lots of rules.
I am a game.
What am I?

Answer: A football game.

Emmanuel Somto Okorogu (6)
Ark John Keats Academy, Enfield

Big And Cute

I have big ears.
I love to eat pears.
I am too big to be your pet but I will always remember you.
I have a long trunk that makes me have fun with water.
What am I?

Answer: An elephant.

Nazli Kendir (5)
Ark John Keats Academy, Enfield

What Am I?

I am part of a game.
People kick me around.
They fight for me sometimes.
They push me into a net.
They play tricks with me and
they score.
What am I?

Answer: A football.

Levi Benjamin (6)
Ark John Keats Academy, Enfield

Who Is He?

He is my best friend.
He is six years old.
He is white.
He doesn't fight.
He likes playing Fortnite.
He watches football.
Who is he?

Answer: Christian.

Elad Danquah (6)
Ark John Keats Academy, Enfield

Animal From Africa

I hunt for my prey.
I roam across Africa.
I have thick hair.
I have gold and brown skin and hair.
I am the king of the jungle.
What am I?

Answer: A lion.

Adam El-Haimer (6)
Ark John Keats Academy, Enfield

Light

I am big and small.
I come in different colours.
I can float in the air.
I come in different shapes.
I am soft and hard.
What am I?

Answer: A balloon.

Aleyna Boran (6)
Ark John Keats Academy, Enfield

The Palace

I am very important.
I am very old and I have many houses.
I live in a palace.
I also live in a castle.
I wear a crown.
Who am I?

Answer: *The Queen*.

Kaiden Campbell (6)
Ark John Keats Academy, Enfield

Red

I grow on a farm.
I am sweet and green, juicy, small and round.
I have a green leaf on top.
I have spots around.
What am I?

Answer: A strawberry.

May Aaliyah Nguyen (6)
Ark John Keats Academy, Enfield

Sweet And Yummy!

I am green outside.
I am pink inside.
I have seeds.
I am juicy and heavy.
I am sweet and yummy.
I am big.
What am I?

Answer: A watermelon.

Elif Agday (6)
Ark John Keats Academy, Enfield

Echo

It is colourful.
It has a beak.
It has wings.
It repeats what you say.
It's sometimes found on a shoulder.
What is it?

Answer: A parrot.

Maysa Testore (6)
Ark John Keats Academy, Enfield

What Am I?

I lived a long time ago.
I am extinct.
I eat meat and other foods.
I am big and tall.
I am scary and loud.
What am I?

Answer: A dinosaur.

Erblin Temaj (5)
Ark John Keats Academy, Enfield

What Am I?

I am your best friend.
My wet nose sniffs for food.
I have four legs and a tail.
I love to play and chase cats.
What am I?

Answer: A dog.

David Oluwasemilore Elegbede (6)
Ark John Keats Academy, Enfield

What Am I?

I am grey.
I thump when I walk.
I drink water from the river.
I have tusks.
I live in the zoo.
What am I?

Answer: An elephant.

Clayton Zefi (5)
Ark John Keats Academy, Enfield

What Am I?

I have three horns to protect myself.
I walk on four heavy legs.
I have a big, bony tail.
I have green, scaly skin to camouflage myself.
I have a hard, bird-like beak to grind up vegetation.
I roamed Earth millions of years ago.
I am a very good defender.
I have a colourful frill.
I have a hard, bony back.
What am I?

Answer: A triceratops.

Aaran Amey (6)
Buckingham Preparatory School, Pinner

Enormous Marble

I am like an orange or a round marble.
I am gigantic, enormous, massive and big.
I am the biggest of eight.
I have lots of really strong gravity.
You can't breathe on me and I am
yellow and white.
I am made of gas.
I am just after the asteroid belt.
What am I?

Answer: Jupiter.

Hassan Faisal (7)
Buckingham Preparatory School, Pinner

Under The Deep Blue Sea

I live underwater.
I never sleep.
I never stop swimming.
You cannot keep me as a pet.
I can smell you from miles away.
When I'm a hundred metres away, I will notice and splash off your feet.
I am not friendly.
What am I?

Answer: A shark.

Hayder Al Mushcab (7)
Buckingham Preparatory School, Pinner

The Dark Shadow

I can run very fast.
You can't hear me.
I can be very cool.
You can't hear my jump.
I use a sharp weapon and it's shiny.
I train at a dojo.
I am the master of fire.
I throw ninja stars.
What am I?

Answer: A ninja.

Jerome Oberoi (7)
Buckingham Preparatory School, Pinner

The Oval Furry Nut

I am brown and furry.
I am hard inside and outside.
I am white inside.
I have a very hard shell that is difficult to break.
I am oval in shape.
People like to drink my cool, refreshing water in the summer.
What am I?

Answer: A coconut.

Anish Kuchangi (6)
Buckingham Preparatory School, Pinner

Fast Pet

I am very fast, almost faster than a car.
I am very strong, an engine's power is measured in my name.
I come in different colours.
I used to be used for work.
I am a big pet.
I have a long mane.
What am I?

Answer: A horse.

Neel Sinha (7)
Buckingham Preparatory School, Pinner

Ferocious Mystery

I have a long, whippy tail.
I have enormous, sharp teeth.
I go fast around animals at night.
I am nocturnal.
I am a carnivore that eats meat.
I am dangerous and furious.
I am prehistoric.
What am I?

Answer: A raptor.

Rishabh Ray (6)
Buckingham Preparatory School, Pinner

A Furry, Scary Beast

I am incredibly scary.
I can be all types of shapes.
I can be harmless or not!
I can be coloured or plain.
I can be enormous or not.
I can live under your bed and scare you.
What am I?

Answer: A monster.

Shrey M Vadera (7)
Buckingham Preparatory School, Pinner

Ring! Ring!

I run on electricity.
I have a camera.
I have a torch to help you see in the dark.
I can make music.
I go *ring, ring, ring, ring!*
What am I?

Answer: A phone.

Maks Pociask (7)
Buckingham Preparatory School, Pinner

Pedestrian Crossing

I have black and white stripes.
I run fast.
I live in South Africa.
I am social and live in small or large groups.
I only eat grass.
What am I?

Answer: A zebra.

Mohsin Faisal (7)
Buckingham Preparatory School, Pinner

Magic

I have a lightning scar.
I come from Muggle Land.
I fly in the sky.
My favourite transport is by train.
I can talk to snakes.
Who am I?

Answer: Harry Potter.

Shivesh Joshi (7)
Buckingham Preparatory School, Pinner

Space

I have a window.
I have a pattern.
People can ride on me.
I am enormous.
I have a flag.
I fly.
What am I?

Answer: An aeroplane.

Ram Tyagi (7)
Buckingham Preparatory School, Pinner

Mountain Or Sea

I have no colour.
I come in a bottle or glass.
I am not an animal.
I can't move.
I can run.
I can't walk.
I make you hydrated.
Your body needs me.
I give you oxygen.
You can eat food for three days,
but you need me.
I am in your washing machine.
You can't live without me.
What am I?

Answer: Water.

Sneha Khurana (7)
Guru Nanak Sikh Academy, Hayes

Stripy Stripes

I live in the wild.
I have orange and black stripes.
When I roar, all the animals run away.
I belong to the mammal family.
I am like a lion but I'm not a lion.
When I hunt, I don't leave my prey alone.
I am fast like a cheetah and a leopard.
What am I?

Answer: A tiger.

Divjot Singh (7)
Guru Nanak Sikh Academy, Hayes

Food

This is children's favourite fast food.
You cut this into slices.
There are yummy toppings on this.
At the end, it has a crust.
It has a circle shape.
Everybody eats this delicious stuff.
We always have this for birthday parties.
What is it?

Answer: A pizza.

Anaikam Sethi (6)
Guru Nanak Sikh Academy, Hayes

Big Friendly Beast

You'll find me in Africa and Asia but there aren't many of us left.
We use to help people as transport and now most of us live in the wild.
I am big but I'm not scary.
I have wrinkly skin but I'm not hairy.
What am I?

Answer: An elephant.

Mehtaab Malhi (7)
Guru Nanak Sikh Academy, Hayes

I'm Juicy

I am a fruit from a hot country.
I grow on trees.
I am a very popular fruit.
I am a fruit with a stone.
My colour is green when unripe and changes to yellow when ripe.
I am used in milkshakes, ice cream and yoghurts.
What am I?

Answer: A mango.

Saihaj Singh Malhotra (6)
Guru Nanak Sikh Academy, Hayes

The Birdhouse

I can be chopped but I'm not a carrot.
I have rings but I'm not an onion.
I can be climbed but I'm not a mountain.
I am made of wood but I'm not a table.
I have a trunk but I'm not a car.
What am I?

Answer: A tree.

Ayush Kumar (6)
Guru Nanak Sikh Academy, Hayes

Slithery Fun

I have scaly skin.
I am very dangerous.
You might get hurt,
If you come too close to me.
So keep away!
I am flat but I don't have wings like a bat.
I have a red tongue and a body.
What am I?

Answer: A snake.

Yafi Muhammad Ajeebkhan (7)
Guru Nanak Sikh Academy, Hayes

What Am I?

I am red and green.
Before I am eaten, I have to be clean.
I grow in summer and spring.
When you see me you'll say "Tin-ting!"
I am juicy.
I love to be eaten by Lucy.
What am I?

Answer: A strawberry.

Anshneev Kaur Arora (6)
Guru Nanak Sikh Academy, Hayes

What Is It?

It has four legs.
It chases cats.
It has a waggly tail.
It likes to eat chicken and meat.
It likes to walk every day.
It barks sometimes because it has lost its chain.
What is it?

Answer: A puppy.

Divleen Kaur Dang (5)
Guru Nanak Sikh Academy, Hayes

Tick-Tock

I have two hands but no feet.
I can be any shape.
I have a face but no eyes.
I tell but I don't talk.
I have numbers around me.
My hands go round and round.
What am I?

Answer: A clock.

Avleen Kaur Virdee (6)
Guru Nanak Sikh Academy, Hayes

Shed On My Head

Shed on my head,
Room where we make bread,
Place where we get fed,
There sits my little bed,
Around all of my teddies,
It's our dream little nest.
What am I?

Answer: A house.

Reet Kaur Chawla (6)
Guru Nanak Sikh Academy, Hayes

Guess If You Can!

I am speedy with two circle shapes.
I come in different colours.
I am noisy but you will feel fresh when you are with me.
Vroom, vroom!
What am I?

Answer: A motorcycle.

Bhagat Singh Vig (6)
Guru Nanak Sikh Academy, Hayes

Fast Run!

I have green, beady eyes.
I have a long tail.
I am very fluffy.
I am very fast.
I have two pointy ears.
I have a pink nose.
What am I?

Answer: A cat.

Eknoor Gill (6)
Guru Nanak Sikh Academy, Hayes

Animal

I am very fast.
I am yellow.
I have brown spots on my body.
I have four legs.
I have a tail.
I live in the forest.
What am I?

Answer: A cheetah.

Prabveer Singh Sachdeva (5)
Guru Nanak Sikh Academy, Hayes

Snow Power

I am white.
I only come in the winter.
If there is a lot of snow, you can play with me.
I sometimes come in different sizes.
What am I?

Answer: A snowman.

Pinak Mistry (7)
Guru Nanak Sikh Academy, Hayes

Fire Wax

In a white coat and a red nose,
The longer it stands, the shorter it grows.
It comes in different colours and shapes.
What is it?

Answer: A candle.

Divjot Singh Khurana (7)
Guru Nanak Sikh Academy, Hayes

The Stripy Animal

I am stripy.
I am a cat.
I am strong.
I have little ears.
I have big whiskers.
My claws are sharp.
What am I?

Answer: A tiger.

Rajdeep Kaur Jheeta (6)
Guru Nanak Sikh Academy, Hayes

What Am I?

I am furry.
I live in Kenya.
I've got a long tail.
I eat meat.
I am a carnivore.
I am fierce.
What am I?

Answer: A lion.

Nanta Singh Matharu (7)
Guru Nanak Sikh Academy, Hayes

Slither Slime

I am long.
I am black in colour.
Children are scared of me.
I live in the forest.
What am I?

Answer: A snake.

Gurleen Dhaliwal (6)
Guru Nanak Sikh Academy, Hayes

Happy Animal

I have sharp teeth.
I have sharp nails.
I have fluffy, ginger fur.
I drink milk.
I like to play with bells.
I eat mice.
What am I?

Answer: A ginger kitten.

Summer Byatt (5)
Harefield Infant School, Harefield

Creepy Cobwebs

I make cobwebs.
I have eight legs.
I am poisonous.
I can climb up walls.
I can catch my food.
I can live inside and outside.
What am I?

Answer: A spider.

Harry John Smith (6)
Harefield Infant School, Harefield

Once Upon A Time

I have a furry coat.
I have a crown.
I am brave.
I can run.
I have a moat.
I live in a castle.
I can read stories.
What am I?

Answer: A princess.

Emilia Peliova (6)
Harefield Infant School, Harefield

Fast

I have sharp claws.
I have sharp teeth.
I have black spots.
I can run fast.
I have yellow fur.
I live in the zoo.
What am I?

Answer: A cheetah.

Lily May Kane (6)
Harefield Infant School, Harefield

A Funny Tale

I get caught by a fisherman's net.
I live in a group.
I can swim.
I hide in corals.
I can be eaten by a shark.
What am I?

Answer: A clownfish.

Molly Moles (6)
Harefield Infant School, Harefield

Black

I have black, thin fur.
I am very fast.
I have very sharp claws.
I have yellow eyes.
I have claws on my feet.
What am I?

Answer: A black panther.

Zayn Kashif-Munir (6)
Harefield Infant School, Harefield

What Am I?

I have claws.
I have eyes.
I have a tail.
I have whiskers.
I have legs.
I have a head.
I go *miaow!*
What am I?

Answer: A cat.

Maisie Hayward (5)
Harefield Infant School, Harefield

Paw Power

I live in a house.
I have a black nose.
I like playing tug of war.
I have four legs.
I have black fur with claws.
What am I?

Answer: A puppy.

Ruby Jockel (5)
Harefield Infant School, Harefield

Big Cat

I have sharp claws.
I am yellow.
I have black spots.
I have sharp teeth.
I have a furry coat.
I eat meat.
What am I?

Answer: A cheetah.

Lilly-Rayne Nuth (6)
Harefield Infant School, Harefield

Purrfect Pet

I can climb trees.
I have black stripes.
I have sharp claws.
I have a tail.
I am fast.
I am good at hiding.
What am I?

Answer: A cat.

Gustas Bartkevicius (5)
Harefield Infant School, Harefield

What Am I?

I have black fur.
I have a ball.
I have four legs.
I have sharp claws.
I eat fish.
I have fluffy fur.
What am I?

Answer: A kitten.

Katie Charlotte Harris (6)
Harefield Infant School, Harefield

Cute

I have sharp claws.
I like to play.
I am very fluffy.
I drink milk.
I like to eat fish.
I can miaow.
What am I?

Answer: A kitten.

Molly Redfern (5)
Harefield Infant School, Harefield

Fast Animal

I have four legs.
I have a tail.
I have fun.
I live in the jungle.
I have yellow fur.
I have claws.
What am I?

Answer: A cheetah.

Amelia Carey (6)
Harefield Infant School, Harefield

Ho, Ho, Ho!

I live on a boat.
I can fight.
I have a cutlass.
I have a pirate hat.
I drink rum.
I bury treasure.
What am I?

Answer: A pirate.

Jake Phillips (6)
Harefield Infant School, Harefield

Climbing Chaos

I am brown.
I like bananas.
I am cheeky.
I like to climb.
I like to hide.
I can swing in the trees.
What am I?

Answer: A monkey.

Betty Ann Shine (6)
Harefield Infant School, Harefield

A Flycatcher

I have eight eyes.
I have eight hairy legs.
I am black.
I am scary.
I am small.
I can spin a web.
What am I?

Answer: A spider.

Olly Hughes (6)
Harefield Infant School, Harefield

What Am I?

I am a pet.
I am furry.
I am good at running.
I can be very big or small.
I eat hay.
I have foals.
What am I?

Answer: A horse.

Francesca Sofflet (6)
Harefield Infant School, Harefield

Games

I tackle people.
I scare girls.
I nutmeg them.
There are eleven players.
There are two goalies.
What am I?

Answer: Football.

Ronny Ford (6)
Harefield Infant School, Harefield

King Bear

I am a type of bear.
I have four legs.
I am black and white.
I eat bamboo.
I live in China.
What am I?

Answer: A panda.

Isabella Gardner (6)
Harefield Infant School, Harefield

Fast Ride

I am fast.
I have two wheels.
I am very big.
I am fun.
I can be red.
I am loud.
What am I?

Answer: A motorbike.

Tyler Josh Sim (6)
Harefield Infant School, Harefield

The Crew

I have a hat.
I have a sharp cutlass.
I have a treasure chest.
I am brave.
I am strong.
What am I?

Answer: A pirate.

Christianna Barnes (6)
Harefield Infant School, Harefield

Once Upon A Time

I have grey skin.
My skin is like armour.
I am very big.
I am rough.
I have one horn.
What am I?

Answer: A rhino.

Hany Abusaid (6)
Harefield Infant School, Harefield

Angry Animal

I have a mane.
I have four legs.
I am the king.
I have yellow fur.
I have sharp claws.
What am I?

Answer: A lion. (upside down)

Harry Seymour (6)
Harefield Infant School, Harefield

What Am I?

I have six legs.
I am spotty.
I have wings.
I am red.
I like sitting on leaves.
What am I?

Answer: A ladybird.

Evie Walford (5)
Harefield Infant School, Harefield

Power

I have two goals.
There are only eleven players.
I am mostly green.
I play with a ball.
What am I?

Answer: Football

Dawsyn Pheney (6)
Harefield Infant School, Harefield

What Am I?

I have claws.
I have a tail.
I have whiskers.
I like milk.
I have kittens.
What am I?

Answer: A cat.

Leo Clements (6)
Harefield Infant School, Harefield

Spotty

I have black spots.
I have really sharp claws.
I have a long tail.
I growl.
What am I?

Answer: A leopard.

Mia Castro-Hendley (6)
Harefield Infant School, Harefield

What Am I?

I've got claws.
I hunt animals.
I am stripy.
I am black and orange.
What am I?

Answer: A tiger.

Riley Huntington (6)
Harefield Infant School, Harefield

What Am I?

I have claws.
I have pointy ears.
I have whiskers.
I have kittens.
What am I?

Answer: A cat.

Lily King (6)
Harefield Infant School, Harefield

What Am I?

I have claws.
I have four legs.
I drink milk.
I have a tail.
What am I?

Answer: A kitten.

Scarlett Brimble (6)
Harefield Infant School, Harefield

Reptiles

I have sharp teeth.
I do not exist.
I can have up to four legs.
What am I?

Answer: A dinosaur.

Ethan Kerry-Wallington (6)
Harefield Infant School, Harefield

Power

I have balls.
There are two goals.
I am mostly green.
What am I?

Answer: A football pitch.

Ben Edwards (6)
Harefield Infant School, Harefield

What Am I?

I have a tail.
I have puppies.
I have fluff.
I have paws.
What am I?

Answer: A dog.

Harley Stokes (6)
Harefield Infant School, Harefield

Slow

I have the ball.
I have black spots.
I have two goals.
What am I?

Answer: Football.

Esra Abusaid (6)
Harefield Infant School, Harefield

What Am I?

I am scaly and small.
I can curl up into a ball.
My tongue is pink and long.
My pong can be very strong.
Ants are my favourite food.
They put me in a happy mood.
I am awake at night,
And like to eat termites.
There aren't many of my type,
So spread the message far and near,
Tell everyone that I am here!
What am I?

Answer: A pangolin.

Emilia Autumn Elizabeth Dennis (6)
Hermitage Primary School, Uxbridge

Poison!

I am a reptile,
But I have no legs!
I can quickly slither across the floor,
So you better run using your legs!
I can poison you so run fast.
I can sometimes be seen as very dangerous.
What am I?

Answer: A snake.

Zain Rahman (6)
Hermitage Primary School, Uxbridge

Human Old Car

I can run a long way.
I am used for racing.
I have four legs.
I can be white, brown or black.
I have long hair on my neck.
I have a thick, hairy tail.
What am I?

Answer: A horse.

Maryam Zelamal (6)
Hermitage Primary School, Uxbridge

What Am I?

I wear a rosy hat,
But have no head.
I'm sharp but have no brain.
I can say anything,
But will never speak a word.
What am I?

Answer: A pencil.

Thomas Santiago Valera (6)
Hermitage Primary School, Uxbridge

The Best Summer Fruit!

I am a yummy fruit and I'm found in many countries.
I am loved by all, from humans to monkeys.
I come in different sizes and I'm delicious to eat.
I grow in summer and I am sweet and sour.
When I'm ready to be eaten, I smell better than a flower.
I have a seed in the centre and it is not brown.
I am the king of fruits but I don't have a crown.
Come on, peel my skin and give me a try!
Close your eyes and tell me, what am I?

Answer: A mango.

Ayushka Shetty (6)
Newton Farm Nursery, Infant & Junior School, South Harrow

Tropical Rio Forest

I have a long, red, narrow and rough tongue.
My tail swirls around.
When I am calm, I stay green.
When I see a female and get excited, I change colour to yellow, orange and red.
I live in a bright and sunny habitat in a tropical rainforest, high up in the trees.
I am a reptile with scaly skin.
I snatch my meals fast with my tongue.
What am I?

Answer: A chameleon.

Sunny Dhanji Khetani (5)
Newton Farm Nursery, Infant & Junior School, South Harrow

The Interesting Person

I don't really exist.
I am extremely magical.
I have a funny type of shoes.
I am funny.
I have buttons on my cardigan.
I have a colourful cardigan.
I am a winged creature.
I have two squares in the middle of my belt.
I have a hat.
I have a nice, colourful dress.
I live in a habitat called a forest.
What am I?

Answer: an elf

Brajesh Pradhan (6)
Newton Farm Nursery, Infant & Junior School, South Harrow

Beautiful!

I am as pretty as ever.
Always coming in different colours.
You may find me in houses and other places but my home is where the sun is.
You all love to smell me but some insects like to use me.
I can be used for different occasions.
Sometimes you put me in your hair for a wedding or to decorate your mansion.
What am I?

Answer: A flower.

Amaal Mamdani (6)
Newton Farm Nursery, Infant & Junior School, South Harrow

Entertaining Place

I am so beautiful.
I am happy in summer.
I am alone in winter.
I am a really enjoyable place.
I have a playing area but I am not a funfair.
People visit me in the summer holidays.
People take a bath on me.
People make fun of me and they eat ice cream.
What am I?

Answer: A beach.

Sagana Satkunarajah (6)
Newton Farm Nursery, Infant & Junior School, South Harrow

Happy Feet

I am black and white but I am not a newspaper.
I can swim but I am not a fish.
I have wings but I can't fly.
I have webbed feet but I'm not a duck.
I live in the snow in the South Pole.
However, you might have seen me in the jungle in Madagascar.
What am I?

Answer: A penguin.

Jasmin Patel (6)
Newton Farm Nursery, Infant & Junior School, South Harrow

One A Day

I am red or green in colour.
I can be made into juice.
I grow on trees.
I can be used for a pie.
I am round like the moon.
I can be tasty, even though I am dry.
I can be a home for little, wriggly worms.
I have lots of vitamin C in me.
What am I?

Answer: An apple.

Samir Yaqubi (6)
Newton Farm Nursery, Infant & Junior School, South Harrow

Tropical Prickle

I come to Britain from a tropical country.
I come round-shaped.
I am prickly on the outside but smooth and sweet inside.
I am not a vegetable but I am delicious and can be eaten, just mind my needles!
I can be enjoyed in rings or pieces.
What am I?

Answer: A pineapple!

Vianna Rabadia-Coll (5)
Newton Farm Nursery, Infant & Junior School, South Harrow

Let's Take To The Sky!

I have a nose but I can't smell.
I have a tail but I am not a mouse.
I can dive but I can't swim.
I have wings but I am not a bird.
We can go on holiday together but I won't stay with you.
Buckle up, it's time to take off!
What am I?

Answer: An aeroplane.

Zara Patel (6)
Newton Farm Nursery, Infant & Junior School, South Harrow

Shinies

I am shiny and glittery.
I look like a spiky, bottomless cylinder.
I have stones on me which are not cheap.
I come from the olden times the most.
I am for very important people.
That important person in the UK is an old lady.
What am I?

Answer: A crown.

Aryan Chaudhary (6)
Newton Farm Nursery, Infant & Junior School, South Harrow

The Iron Lady

I go from one place to another.
I am long.
I have lots of doors and windows.
I am fun to ride on.
I pass through a tunnel or I go over a bridge.
I have wheels but I can't ride on a road.
What am I?

Answer: A train.

Simran Kalra (5)
Newton Farm Nursery, Infant & Junior School, South Harrow

I Am A Sweet Fruit!

I am a fruit.
I am not a berry.
I am delicious.
I am found in shops.
I have tiny seeds.
I come in different sizes.
I am very juicy.
Some people think I'm yummy.
What am I?

Answer: A strawberry.

Jeeya Prasai (6)
Newton Farm Nursery, Infant & Junior School, South Harrow

White

You would like to make me when it's cold.
I will make you freeze if you don't wear gloves.
I have a round face, an orange nose and a rocky smile.
I have brown arms.
What am I?

Answer: A snowman. (upside down)

Sahasra Myneni (6)
Newton Farm Nursery, Infant & Junior School, South Harrow

On A Snowy Day

You can see me in winter.
I do not have any legs.
I can't live for one hundred days.
I do not wear any dresses.
People like me but it is difficult to hug me.
What am I?

Answer: A snowman.

Maryam Shifan (6)
Newton Farm Nursery, Infant & Junior School, South Harrow

Farmer's Helper

I can fly.
I eat nectar from flowers.
I am a beautiful creature.
I have wide wings.
I have two antennae.
I carry pollen from flower to flower.
What am I?

Answer: A butterfly.

Sivika Arulkumaran (5)
Newton Farm Nursery, Infant & Junior School, South Harrow

In The Sky

I am tiny but there are many of me.
I am only seen in the dark.
I am shiny.
I have five sides.
I am in a nursery rhyme.
Everyone can see me.
What am I?

Answer: A star.

Sophia Iqbal (6)
Newton Farm Nursery, Infant & Junior School, South Harrow

Fruit And Veggies

It is red.
It is juicy.
You get it from Sainsbury's.
There are seeds on it.
It is sweet.
It is in a packet.
What is it?

Answer: A strawberry.

Jasmin Aarushi Patel (6)
Newton Farm Nursery, Infant & Junior School, South Harrow

Little Soft Bloom

I come in different colours.
I am soft.
I have four sides, which means four right angles.
I am made with cotton.
What am I?

Answer: A mat.

Dhanvi (6)
Newton Farm Nursery, Infant & Junior School, South Harrow

The Grinder

I am white.
I am shiny.
I chatter at times.
I can grow and I can fall while I am grinding to make things soft.
What am I?

Answer: Teeth.

Akanksha Vydyam (6)
Newton Farm Nursery, Infant & Junior School, South Harrow

Something Special

I'm as pretty as a bird.
I'm not a fly but I fly in the air.
I'm very cute as well.
I'm not furry at all.
I'm skinny and short.
You will not find me at night,
only when it's day.
You might find me in the jungle.
My tummy doesn't glow
and doesn't rumble.
I'm small and sweet,
and I don't eat meat.
The word starts with 'butter',
and ends with 'fly'.
What am I?

Answer: A butterfly.

Dalia Al-Jubouri (7)
Oakington Manor Primary School, Wembley

Nature

I am white but I'm not a cloud.
I am cold but I'm not hail.
I come down to the ground but I'm not rain.
I come after autumn but I'm not spring.
You can make people out of me but not real people.
You can throw me but if I am small, I'll melt.
I am cold so you need gloves, a scarf and a hat.
I turn runny as I get old.
I turn into an icicle when it gets really cold.
What am I?

Answer: Snow.

Diyani Vekeria (6)
Oakington Manor Primary School, Wembley

What Am I?

I have very short ears.
I have got a long tail.
I have got four long legs.
I have got small eyes.
I have a tiny nose.
I am a pet for people.
I have very sharp nails.
People stroke me.
I have a lovely voice.
I can run very fast, no one can catch me.
I am a very harmless creature so I don't bite people.
If someone hurts me very badly, then I run away very fast.
What am I?

Answer: A cat.

Aksheran Ananthaseran (7)
Oakington Manor Primary School, Wembley

Rubbish Picker

We come in all different sizes
and all different colours.
I like to pick up some little stuff.
I am very noisy but some can be quiet.
I like to work in the day but I can also work at night.
I can break if I make contact with water.
What am I?

Answer: A vacuum cleaner.

Cianna Howe-Young (7)
Oakington Manor Primary School, Wembley

Bow-Wow

I can be in the wild sometimes or a pet.
Sheep feel safe around me when
I guard them.
You can find me in PAW Patrol.
I like chasing cats and birds.
I like burying bones.
My favourite thing is to go on long
walks with my owner.
What am I?

Answer: A dog.

Ihsaan Agyeman-Owens (6)
Oakington Manor Primary School, Wembley

Up And Down

I go up when the rain comes down.
I come in different colours.
I come in different sizes.
The top of me is delicate.
I go up when it's sunny too.
I've existed for many centuries.
What am I?

Answer: An umbrella.

Maximilian Paulo Lule (7)
Oakington Manor Primary School, Wembley

Pets

I have different colours.
I am hunted by a fox.
I have pointed ears and fur
and I eat carrots.
I am cute and jump about.
I can sometimes mess up
but everybody loves me.
What am I?

Answer: A bunny.

Farhan Ahmad Saiady (6)
Oakington Manor Primary School, Wembley

Digital World

I am black, grey and white.
You can play with me.
I can help you study.
You can fold me and put me in your bag.
I have a keyboard and a mouse.
Use the Internet but be safe.
What am I?

Answer: A laptop.

Kitty Lauter (6)
Oakington Manor Primary School, Wembley

Colours

I have lots of colours.
I am very high in the sky.
I don't come out all the time.
You only see me in certain places.
Sometimes I come in twos.
I have a song about me.
What am I?

Answer: A rainbow.

Aysia Demetrio Patel (6)
Oakington Manor Primary School, Wembley

Blossoming Beauty

My thorns are like a sword.
My drink comes from the Lord.
I am beautiful and red but without water,
I'm dead.
I grow from the ground.
The wind makes me sway around.
What am I?

Answer: A rose.

Romario Jozef Scoon (7)
Oakington Manor Primary School, Wembley

Sun And Fun

I am nice and hot.
I like to get wet.
People always sweat.
Ice cream is my treat.
People are going to the beach.
I am full of joy.
I hope you will enjoy!
What am I?

Answer: Summer.

Amelia Sarban (7)
Oakington Manor Primary School, Wembley

Wet, Wet, Wet

I am big and blue.
You pull me to get through me.
You climb to get out of me.
I am deep and shallow.
You can dive into me.
1, 2, 3, turn and breathe!
What am I?

Answer: A swimming pool.

Elijah Vernalls (6)
Oakington Manor Primary School, Wembley

What Fruit Am I?

I'm a fruit.
I'm as red as blood.
I'm small but I'm not a ball.
I don't speak or move but I'm tasty.
My leaves are not for eating.
What am I?

Answer: A strawberry.

Sarah Dumitriu (7)
Oakington Manor Primary School, Wembley

Floater

I float around in space.
It is a really nice place.
I have a rocket.
I don't have pockets.
I have an air tank.
I don't work for the bank.
What am I?

Answer: An astronaut.

Mohemed Ahmad (7)
Oakington Manor Primary School, Wembley

Cool Breeze

I am round in shape.
I have flaps.
I run when switched on.
I don't have legs.
I stand on the floor.
I make you cool.
What am I?

Answer: An electric fan.

Dev Shaju Nair (6)
Oakington Manor Primary School, Wembley

Important Person

I live in a castle.
I am one of the most respected people.
I am in charge of everybody.
I wear a crown.
I am from the royal family.
Who am I?

Answer: *The Queen.*

Asma Hassan (7)
Oakington Manor Primary School, Wembley

My House

I have a hard shell.
I have four legs.
I can put my head under my shell.
I walk very slowly.
When I am scared, I hide in my shell.
What am I?

Answer: A turtle.

Raine Denae Robinson (7)
Oakington Manor Primary School, Wembley

Gentle Pal

I have a long neck.
I am the size of a tree.
I eat leaves.
I have a long, great tongue.
I live in a zoo.
I am quite tall.
What am I?

Answer: A giraffe.

Samira Said (5)
Oakington Manor Primary School, Wembley

Speed

I am quick and speedy.
You don't really need me.
I am silly but I am not a spy.
I wear a mask.
I always share a task.
What am I?

Answer: A ninja.

Abdullahi Ahmad (6)
Oakington Manor Primary School, Wembley

The Amazing Animal

I have very long legs.
I love to eat grass and straw and leaves.
I live in Africa but you may see me in the zoo.
I have a mane but I am not a horse.
I can gallop faster than a cheetah.
I have black and white stripes like a zebra crossing.
What am I?

Answer: A zebra.

Samaiah Marlene Bent (6)
St James' CE Primary School, Enfield

The Creepy, Scary Animal

I have a long, green mouth with black spots.
I have a very long tail.
I move gracefully when I'm walking.
I have to eat meat because I'm a carnivore.
I live in a big ocean because there are lots of creatures and I am one of them.
What am I?

Answer: A crocodile.

Rhema Zoe Banful (6)
St James' CE Primary School, Enfield

The Bumpy, Long Animal

I have razor-sharp teeth that cut like knives.
My hiss is so loud it could deafen you.
My skin is scary and bumpy to touch.
I eat glorious meat.
I can be the size of a long boat.
I live in a dirty swamp, waiting for my prey.
What am I?

Answer: A crocodile.

Emily Tuffour (6)
St James' CE Primary School, Enfield

The Bad Animal

I like to swim around in the swamp searching for food.
I have scaly skin that is rough to touch.
My teeth are razor-sharp.
I only eat meat, fish and sometimes humans.
I love to sit in the sunshine and feel the heat.
What am I?

Answer: A crocodile.

Isabel Ibrahim (6)
St James' CE Primary School, Enfield

The Fastest Runner

I have a beautiful mane but I am not a horse.
I live in a herd.
I am a herbivore and I love to eat tall grass.
I can run extremely fast.
I live in the African wilderness.
I am a black and white, stripy animal.
What am I?

Answer: A zebra.

Malakai Amali Rowland (6)
St James' CE Primary School, Enfield

Scary Animal

I have bright, green eyes that glow in the dark.
My fur is soft but you cannot stroke me.
My teeth can tear into meat.
I look like a cat but I am wild.
I live in Africa.
I have orange and black, stripy fur.
What am I?

Answer: A tiger.

Chigozie Jessy Anyanwu (6)
St James' CE Primary School, Enfield

The Happy Animal

I can move really fast, especially when I am chasing my dinner.
I can roar so loudly it can burst your eardrums!
I have a long, furry tail.
I only eat juicy meat.
I live in the scorching desert.
What am I?

Answer: A tiger.

Evangelina Duzgun (6)
St James' CE Primary School, Enfield

Terrifying Animal

I walk around.
I eat grass.
I have a long tail.
I dig under the ground.
I hop around.
I have white and black colours.
I eat plants, I eat flowers.
I have scary claws.
What am I?

Answer: A tiger.

Naomi Oprer (6)
St James' CE Primary School, Enfield

The Creepy Animal

I have two sharp teeth.
I have green, scaly skin.
I can swim underwater.
I eat other animals.
I am massive.
I have sharp spikes all over my back.
What am I?

Answer: A crocodile.

Ocean-Maxime Asiamah (6)
St James' CE Primary School, Enfield

The Terrifying Animal

I am a part of the cat family.
I am all different colours.
I have orange and black stripes.
I am famous.
I can move slow and fast.
I eat meat.
What am I?

Answer: A tiger.

Ayla-Rae (6)
St James' CE Primary School, Enfield

The Creepy, Scary Animal

I have bright green skin.
I have a long tail.
I move very, very slowly in the wet, green swamp because I need to get my dinner.
I swim in the swamp.
What am I?

Answer: A crocodile.

Arav Guddah (6)
St James' CE Primary School, Enfield

Stripy Riddle

I have little ears.
I have four legs.
I am a bit fluffy.
I can run fast.
I like to hunt.
I am massive.
I have a black nose.
What am I?

Answer: A zebra.

Audrey Tawiah (5)
St James' CE Primary School, Enfield

The Fab Animal

I am white and black.
I am fast.
I am in a family and I am a herbivore.
I am fast and I am stripy.
I am slow and I am in the grass.
What am I?

Answer: A zebra.

Ademidola Akarakiri (5)
St James' CE Primary School, Enfield

What Am I?

I have long ears.
I have a small tail.
I have long whiskers.
I have four legs.
I eat carrots and broccoli.
What am I?

Answer: A rabbit.

Taylan Kiani (6)
St James' CE Primary School, Enfield

The Terrible Animal

I have four legs.
I am fast like a tiger.
I live in Africa.
I am stripy.
I am black and white.
What am I?

Answer: A zebra.

Vasianna Dussard (6)
St James' CE Primary School, Enfield

What Am I?

I have a long, furry tail.
I like to sniff a lot.
I have long, soft fur like cotton wool.
What am I?

Answer: A dog.

Joel Jojo (5)
St James' CE Primary School, Enfield

Vicious Predator

I have wings as light as feathers.
I am viciously dangerous and as fast as a bullet train.
I love sucking red juice out of you.
My skin is silky.
I am as black as coal.
You will find me in wet, dark places.
When I come, you will freak out!
If you see my family, you will jump out of bed.
What am I?

Answer: A vampire bat.

Millan Babrah (7)
St Mary's CE School, Norwood Green

Calling All Bakers

I am light brown.
I have a spotty wrapper underneath me.
I have rainbow whipped cream on me.
I have sprinkles on me.
I am as tasty as a big, rainbow lollipop.
I always love to be in different kinds of boxes.
I come in different colours and shapes.
What am I?

Answer: A cupcake.

Abigail Roman (7)
St Mary's CE School, Norwood Green

The Hotter Evening

In the evening, the cold winter is leaving me.
The days are getting longer as the tree branches get stronger and stronger.
Getting ready to bear scrumptious fruit, colourful flowers are blooming.
The sun is looming, ready for this day.
What am I?

Answer: Spring.

Parisa Rizvi (7)
St Mary's CE School, Norwood Green

The Great Runner

I'm soft and I have dark grey spots.
I'm as fast as a flash.
I can run up to a hundred miles.
I like to eat meat, juicy and succulent.
I am a predator who can find its prey in the bushes too.
I am fierce.
What am I?

Answer: A cheetah.

Ilaria Bhatti (7)
St Mary's CE School, Norwood Green

A Shorter Friend

I can grow or I can be short.
I can be painted or I can stay plain.
I can be square or a circle.
If you want, you can cut me but not to the end!
I am pink, white, hard and fat.
I am as smooth as a pebble in the sea.
What am I?

Answer: A nail.

Giovanna Armond (7)
St Mary's CE School, Norwood Green

The Cheeky Friend

I am as brown as a sausage.
I swing from branch to branch.
I am as cheeky as an elephant.
I am a bit heavy.
I am as fast as lightning.
I am as jumpy as a kangaroo.
I have been alive since God made the world.
What am I?

Answer: A monkey.

Arran Singh Reehal
St Mary's CE School, Norwood Green

Is It Pretty?

I am beautiful and pretty and as light as a feather.
I can fly very high, I float in the sky.
I am very delicate and talented.
I live for only a few weeks.
I am as patterned as a beautiful rug.
I love flowers!
What am I?

Answer: A butterfly.

Summer Zahra Rizvi (7)
St Mary's CE School, Norwood Green

A Fierce Predator

I am as cool as a tiger.
I am as black as coal.
I am as strong as the Hulk.
I am as skinny as a pencil.
My bodysuit is as glimmery as a sunset.
I am as fast as a cheetah.
I flash through your eyes.
Who am I?

Answer: Black Panther.

Harry Alan Burns
St Mary's CE School, Norwood Green

The Great Looker

I am a fierce predator.
You can see me in the open sea.
I like tasty, humongous fish.
I carry jumpy rabbits.
I live in the highest home.
I am America's dangerous animal.
I am the king of the birds.
What am I?

Answer: An eagle.

Daniel Joshua Wilson-Paz Sotomayor (7)
St Mary's CE School, Norwood Green

Put Me On!

You put me on when it's dark and cold.
Adults and children wear me because I am warm.
Nearly everyone in the world has me!
I have many colours.
Everyone loves me.
People put me on when it's winter.
What am I?

Answer: A jacket.

Jessica Toms (7)
St Mary's CE School, Norwood Green

The Colourful Cute!

I am colourful and cute.
I am funny and I scratch.
I love to dance and I drink milk.
I am as soft as a cushion.
I have big, soft ears.
I have legs as fluffy as wool.
I have whiskers and I am alive.
What am I?

Answer: A kitten.

Niam Bangar (7)
St Mary's CE School, Norwood Green

Yummy, Scrummy In Your Tummy

I am a yummy thing that you can lick and bite.
I can be any flavour or any shape.
I can be on a stick or in a bowl.
I am very cold.
I can be eaten all year round.
If I am left in the sun, I will melt.
What am I?

Answer: Ice cream.

Alisha Patel
St Mary's CE School, Norwood Green

Royalty

I love to wear shiny shoes and carry my expensive handbag.
I walk all my dogs with my family.
I have a pretty house.
I love spending time with my family.
I have butlers to serve food and open the doors.
Who am I?

Answer: *The Queen.*

Mya Belle Spencer
St Mary's CE School, Norwood Green

The Nice Thing

The sun is very fun.
People like going to the beach when it is my turn.
People love me very much.
People usually relax.
People don't like going to the beach when I go.
I don't like going.
What am I?

Answer: Summer.

Renu Kaur Virdee (7)
St Mary's CE School, Norwood Green

The Scary Animal

I am as fast as a cheetah.
I am as large as a truck.
I am a flying animal.
I am as big as a big skyscraper.
I eat big sea creatures.
I am as young as a rock.
I am smooth.
What am I?

Answer: A pterodactyl.

Jarvis Isaac Sylvester Dennis (7)
St Mary's CE School, Norwood Green

A Jumping Thing

I live in a zoo with my friends.
I can be fun.
As a pet, I can walk with my owner.
I can see but I can't talk.
I have a mouth to eat.
I can eat leaves.
I can jump high.
What am I?

Answer: A monkey.

Dhruv Jahnaid Vansanten (7)
St Mary's CE School, Norwood Green

The Valuable

I'm more valuable than gold.
I don't cost a penny.
I'm hard to find but easy to lose.
I'm very handy.
I help a lot of people.
I'm so sweet and kind.
What am I?

Answer: A friend.

Anika Jagota (7)
St Mary's CE School, Norwood Green

A Man's Friend

I am as slippery as a shiny table.
I make everything.
I am as funny as a clown.
I cook any type of food.
I do anything that I am asked.
I talk in a weird way.
What am I?

Answer: A robot.

Richard Clarke (7)
St Mary's CE School, Norwood Green

The Sea

I am as orange as an orange.
I live at the bottom of the sea.
A diver might see me.
I can stick to the sand.
I am very hard to find.
I feed on the seabed.
What am I?

Answer: A starfish.

Eleanor Hamlyn (6)
St Mary's CE School, Norwood Green

Mr T

You put me where there is meat.
I am very scary because I have sharp teeth.
I stomp loudly because I have big feet.
My arms are too short to reach my face.
What am I?

Answer: A T-rex.

Jeevan Singh Sanghera (6)
St Mary's CE School, Norwood Green

Est.1991

YOUNG WRITERS INFORMATION

We hope you have enjoyed reading this book – and that you will continue to in the coming years.

If you're a young writer who enjoys reading and creative writing, or the parent of an enthusiastic poet or story writer, do visit our website **www.youngwriters.co.uk**. Here you will find free competitions, workshops and games, as well as recommended reads, a poetry glossary and our blog.

If you would like to order further copies of this book, or any of our other titles, then please give us a call or visit **www.youngwriters.co.uk**.

Young Writers
Remus House
Coltsfoot Drive
Peterborough
PE2 9BF
(01733) 890066
info@youngwriters.co.uk